What People Are Saying About Pamela Yellen...

"Pamela Yellen should definitely win a Nobel Prize. With her guidance, you can grow a nest egg into a small fortune without the risks of conventional investments and political uncertainty."

–JOSEPH SUGARMAN, Entrepreneur, Author, and BluBlocker Corporation Founder

"The founder of our company, Martin Edelston, lived by this credo: 'The only things worth talking about are the things you can't talk about.' Thank goodness Pamela Yellen lives by that same credo and has made it her life's mission to buck conventional wisdom when it comes to the critical issues every consumer faces as they struggle to not outlive their money."

–BRIAN KURTZ, Founder of Titans Marketing and Former Executive Vice President, Boardroom, Inc

"The Bank On Yourself system may not be the only way to invest your hard-earned money, but it is by far the *safest* and *surest* way to maintain your nest egg and grow it steadily. Keep yourself and your family safe from the greed of Wall Street and the banking system."

–DR. TIMOTHY ZELKO, Cosmetic Surgeon

"Most financial 'experts' make the simple complex; Pamela Yellen does just the opposite. Her advice to our readers always has been spot-on. Many people are many thousands of dollars richer thanks to her."

–WAYNE M. BARRETT, Publisher and Editor-in-Chief, USA Today Magazine

"Traditional finance advice just doesn't work anymore. Things have changed, and Pamela Yellen is the first to find ways to teach others to secure their financial futures and become financially free in this new and confusing world."

NICKY LAMARCO, Writer and "The Review Mom"

RE$CUE YOUR RETIREMENT

Five Wealth-Killing Traps of 401(k)s, IRAs and Roth Plans—and How to Avoid Them!

PAMELA YELLEN
NEW YORK TIMES BEST-SELLING AUTHOR

Printed in the United States of America

10 9 8 7 6 5 4 3 2

ISBN-13: 978-0-578-53104-5 (trade paper)

Legal Disclaimer: While a great deal of care has been taken to provide accurate and current information regarding the subject matter covered, neither the author, Pamela Yellen, nor any others involved in the creation of this book, are responsible for any errors or omissions, or for the results obtained from the use of this book. The information contained in this book is intended to provide general information and does not constitute financial or legal advice. See General Disclaimer on p. 84.

BANK ON YOURSELF®
GROW AND PROTECT YOUR FINANCIAL FUTURE

A Bank On Yourself Publication

www.BankOnYourself.com

Send feedback to support@bankonyourself.com

This book is dedicated to my husband Larry Hayward who has been my rock for 30 years in both good times and bad, supporting and believing in me more than I sometimes believe in myself.

Contents

Introduction

People just haven't saved enough for retirement. And they're going to outlive their money.

—SALLIE KRAWCHECK,
former President, Global Wealth and Investment Management, Bank of America

WHEN YOU were a kid being scolded for some hair-brained scheme, did your mom ever say, "Just because every other kid in town jumps off a cliff, does that mean you should do it too?" Remember the old Roadrunner cartoons? Well, if you've been following the conventional "wisdom" for your retirement planning, odds are you're headed toward one of those Wiley Coyote splats from a 500-foot fall.

And this will happen *despite* the fact that you've been conscientious about contributing to your retirement plan, *despite* the fact that you have been "doing all the right things" financially, *despite* the fact that you are one smart, savvy cookie in most areas of life.

At retirement, Roadrunner is still gonna get you.

You may have had an inkling of this truth. You may have pushed your retirement age back a few years. You may have started to downsize your expectations about the lifestyle you'll be able to live in retirement.

You may have spent a few restless nights calculating and recalculating just how much money you'll have during your elder years and exactly what that looks like (less like gourmet candlelit dinners in Cancun and more like tuna sandwiches on the back porch). Or maybe you've seen your retirement account tank in the market, had a medical emergency drain what you had saved, or lost your job which ended your career way earlier than you had planned.

You're not alone. As Robert J. Shiller, Professor of Economics, at Yale University noted...

> **"Errors of human judgment can infect even the smartest people, thanks to overconfidence, lack of attention to details, and excessive trust in the judgments of others, stemming from a failure to understand that *others are not making independent judgments,* but are themselves following still others—the blind leading the blind."**

I know, I know. This book will probably make you *extremely* uncomfortable.

You might feel more than a little squeamish to hear about all the leaks, rats, and rotting hull of the financial ship you've built with your blood, sweat, tears and dollars. You might get angry, anxious and confused to realize that you've built your financial future and retirement on a house of cards (known as conventional Wall Street-based retirement plans) that can come tumbling down at any time through no fault of your own.

I take no joy in saying it, but I'm the bearer of bad tidings.

But if you can get through all the fear, angst and anger these bad tidings may cause you, I've got some *good* news for you as well. And if you can hang in there and keep an open mind, I can show you how to turn your rotting financial ship into a sleek, secure sailing vessel.

In this short book, I'm going to help you understand exactly why the Economic Policy Institute said in its report on The State of American Retirement: "The shift from pensions to 401(k)s has failed the majority of American workers." I'll give you stats about the ugly results that conventional retirement plans (401(k)s, IRAs, 403(b)s, etc.) have produced for so many. I'm going to show you why your life in retirement will likely last *longer* than you think it will, *cost far more* than you've planned for, and why you need to take a *different approach* to avoid outliving your money.

And I'll give you questions to ask yourself to help you estimate the financial fiasco you might face in retirement if you stay on your current path.

Yeah, the first part of this book may be painful to read. But it will arm you with facts and strategies you need so you don't wake up one morning, ready to retire but without enough money to do so.

Next, I'll expose the **five wealth-killing traps of conventional retirement plans**, such as 401(k)s, IRAs, 403(b)s and Roth plans. You're probably not even aware of these traps. Or if you are aware of them, you've been told by everyone—your financial advisor, your plan administrator, and your dentist—that these traps are just unavoidable, necessary evils on the road to retirement (they aren't). And it's *not* too late to do something about it. I'm going to reveal exactly how these traps are putting your future in jeopardy and eroding the financial security you've struggled to build, leaving you vulnerable despite your best efforts.

Okay, so this part isn't a barrel of laughs either.

However, after I explain these five devastating traps of your conventional retirement plan(s), I'm going to reveal how to avoid them. I'll show you a time-tested option that's been around much longer and has produced much better and more consistent and predictable results than those government-sponsored conventional plans you've been putting your hard-earned dollars into. It's a strategy that has helped literally hundreds of thousands of families achieve their retirement and financial goals and dreams without taking *any* unnecessary risks. This is the fun part!

But we need to get through the rough stuff first ...

CHAPTER ONE

Uncomfortable Truths about Conventional Retirement Plans

"Prediction is very difficult, especially if it's about the future."

—NEILS BOHR, Nobel Prize-winning physicist

I HAVE NO idea what the economic climate will be as you read this book. Absolutely no clue. We could be in a screaming bull market, or in the throes of a financial crash and recession, or somewhere in between. And the truth is, *nobody else knows either.*

Since 2000, we've already had two stock market crashes of 50% or more. Warren Buffett, the Oracle of Omaha and arguably the savviest investor of all time, had this to say in his 2018 annual shareholder's letter:

> "Stock market losses of 50% or more are not only possible but inevitable in the future... No one can tell you when these will happen. The light can at any time go from green to red without pausing at yellow."

Do you really think the market will never crash again? Or that you'll have enough warning to get out if it does?

As I write this, we're in the longest running bull market in history and the first *ever* to hit its tenth birthday! This would be great news if it weren't for the fact that, historically, the longest bull markets have ended with a bang, not a whimper...

The critical question is: How much does your retirement depend on the stock market, a beast that you can't predict or control? If your funds are in a conventional retirement plan, the answer is usually "nearly 100%."

Before we get into a brief history of how we got into this mess, let me point out the critical difference between "saving" and "investing." *Saving* is what you do with money you *can't afford to lose*, so you know for sure that the money will be there when you need it. *Investing* is what you can do with money you *can afford to lose*. You throw it on a craps table in Vegas or on the Wall Street roulette wheel. You're taking a big risk, with the hope of making a big gain.

Now let me ask you: Is the money in your retirement accounts money you can afford to lose? Probably not. So, if you *can't* afford to lose it, should you be *investing* that money or *saving* it? Well, if you're in a conventional retirement plan and you're like most people, you are most likely "investing" your hard-earned life's savings in...

The Wall Street Casino

We've been told again and again that to get our money to "work" for us, to build a sizable nest egg and get a rate of return that will outpace inflation, we *must* invest in the stock market and be willing to accept its inherent risks. How many times have you heard that the stock market is the best place to grow your nest egg? I will prove to you that this is a myth that Wall Street has brainwashed us into. Wall Street grudgingly admits there are no guarantees that your investment account won't lose some—or all!—of its value in any given year. But let's look beyond that statement to the heart-stopping reality: In the two market crashes we've had so far since 2000, many people lost a full 50% or more of their retirement funds.

Most people don't realize or remember how long it can take the stock market to recover after a crash. Since 1929 we've had *three* market crashes where the Dow took between 16 and 25 years to return to pre-crash levels.

Could something like that happen again? Who knows? And that's the problem. So the big question to ask yourself is (in the immortal words of Dirty Harry): "Are ya feelin' lucky?"

Since 1929 we've had *three* market crashes where the Dow took between 16 and 25 years to return to pre-crash levels.

Can you even imagine the impact on your own plans for retirement if you end up having to wait 25 years for the market to recover?

Really, how enthusiastic are you about gambling with the funds you'll need when you're no longer working? Here's a quick test to measure it: What is the *minimum* acceptable annual return you'd want to get that would make you willing to stomach the nerve-wracking volatility of the stock market? 7%? 10%? Maybe even more? I've surveyed thousands of people, and almost everyone says they wouldn't go through the agony if they got only 5%.

Okay, so how is that playing out? As I write this, the 2019 DALBAR report[1] just came out—and it's not good news for investors. According to the report, the typical equity mutual fund investor has earned *only* 3.88% annually for the past 20 years, beating inflation for that period by only *1.7%* a year. Asset allocation and fixed income investors actually *lost ground* when factoring in inflation.

So, if most people wouldn't put up with the stomach-churning, unpredictability of the stock market for an annual return of 5%, how come so many people are accepting a real annual return of less than 2%?

...the typical equity mutual fund investor has earned only 3.88% annually for the past 20 years, beating inflation for that period by only 1.7% a year.

Wait! If the market can be so unpredictable and the returns so minimal, how did so many of us come to risk our retirement funds in the Wall Street Casino? Well, an interesting thing happened on the way to retirement...

A Brief History: The Fix That's Broken

Before 1978, your grandfather's or great-grandfather's employer *promised* him a certain amount of money every month in retirement for as long as he lived. Those plans are called pension plans. The technical name is "defined benefit plans." The benefits you were to receive were defined and laid out in advance. Unless something totally catastrophic happened, those benefits were *guaranteed*. But these days, pension plans are as rare as the Northern Hairy-Nosed Wombat. (These critters do exist, but they're *very* rare.)

Even if you are one of the lucky few participating in a company pension plan, keep reading. Sadly, those plans are in danger too. According to the Federal Reserve, in spite of the long bull market, pensions (public and private combined) are underfunded by about

27% in a time when hordes of people with pensions are entering or approaching retirement!

In 1978, Congress added Section 401(k) to the tax code, creating a tax-deferred way for employees to *augment* their pensions. These plans were *never* intended to replace company pension plans, but that's exactly what happened. At one time, 80% of private sector workers who had a workplace retirement plan had a pension fund. But according to the Bureau of Labor Statistics, by 2017, only 18% of private sector workers had access to a company pension and just 15% of people participated in one.

Companies figured out that it's cheaper to offer a small matching contribution to an employee's 401(k) plan than to fund and pay for the management of a company pension plan. So they transferred the burden of funding employees' retirement to the employees themselves.

That would be us.

If you are an employee today, your company very likely offers a 401(k), 403(b), or similar plan. The funds in that plan are typically invested in the Wall Street Casino, that thing that you can't control or predict. Technically, these plans are called "defined contribution plans," but the more accurate name is "hope and pray" plans.

Even the "Father of the 401(k)" Has Disowned It

I hate to dash those hopes and disappoint those prayers, but you should know that even the man who's considered to be the Father of the 401(k) now despises the whole system! Ted Benna, who three decades ago seized on an IRS loophole to transform American retirement savings, thinks he created a monster. As Benna told MarketWatch in 2011, he believes the 401(k) "*monster is out of control...It is far beyond what most participants were able to deal with... We're throwing tons of money away trying to teach participants how to become skilled investors ... but it just hasn't worked... I would blow up the system and restart with something totally different.*" (Apparently, Mr. Benna and Dr. Frankenstein had similar qualms about their creations.)

Benna says he watched Wall Street and Big Business over the years pervert the 401(k) in ways he couldn't possibly predict. In a more recent interview, Ted Benna discussed three reasons why we should be very leery of *both* 401(k)s and IRAs:

- Wall Street has hijacked these plans, and the **excessive fees** charged by mutual fund companies and plan administrators are **robbing you of up to half of your nest egg** (more on this in a bit).
- Benna believes the next stock and bond market crash is imminent and *could wipe out 40%* of the typical portfolio.
- The government may repeal the 401(k) and IRA, so you won't be able to put any more money pre-tax into these accounts, or the amount you can put in will be drastically reduced (Congress considers doing this every few years!).

Spoiler Alert! The vehicle Ted Benna says he now uses for most of his *own* nest egg is the same strategy I'll show you in this book!

As labor economist and nationally recognized retirement security expert Professor Teresa Ghilarducci notes, "We've run the [401(k)] experiment for 40 years. We pronounce it a failure."

Wait a minute! Haven't we been told again and again that 401(k)s and IRAs are the best way to save for a comfortable retirement? Doesn't our government legislate and bless those plans and even allow us to defer paying taxes on our contributions? (At least under current tax law.) Our employers set them up for us and often even give us matching funds when we contribute. What's not to like about matching funds? It *must* be good for us, right?

When Free Money Isn't Really Free

That employer match is almost irresistible, isn't it? It's like Santa filling your stocking because you've been a good little girl or boy. But is your employer really that magnanimous?

The Center for Retirement Research did a study revealing that for every dollar an employer contributes to your 401(k) match, they pay *90 cents less* in salary to men and *99 cents less* to women on average. Translation: For every matching dollar you're given, you *really* only receive 10 cents or less in total compensation.[2] Plus, you don't even get all of your employer match until you're "vested," usually after 4 to 6 years on the job. If you leave your job or get laid off before then, you typically don't get the full match—and in some companies, you lose it all! But here's a fun fact: According to the Bureau of Labor Statistics, the average time people stay on the job is only *4.2 years*!

So, you're really netting *pennies*, not dollars, in matching funds *plus* you'll lose some or all of this pittance if you don't stick around longer than the average worker. That match is sounding more and more like a lump of coal, isn't it?

So, you're really netting *pennies,* not dollars, in matching funds *plus* you'll lose some or all of this pittance if you don't stick around longer than the average worker.

In 401(k) plans, your company administers the plan, makes its match (when times are good), then washes its hands regarding the outcome. Your employer offers you a plan and—thanks to the law Congress passed—often even invests your retirement funds *without* your permission. Oh, and then, if those investments tank, in most cases, your employer can't be held responsible. Hmmm. Not sounding quite so good, is it?

Today's government-approved retirement plans offer absolutely *no guarantees*. Okay, that's not exactly true. They *do* guarantee that brokers, mutual fund managers, and fat cats on Wall Street are *always* going to make money, no matter how much money *you* lose! *So, someone is always making money. That somebody just doesn't happen to be you.*

For many participants, the plans that started replacing pension plans after 1978 have been less effective than stuffing cash in a mattress. Thanks to this shift from guaranteed company pensions to "do-it-yourself" 401(k)s and IRAs, the responsibility for saving enough for retirement has shifted squarely onto your shoulders. So how's that working out?

- The typical household nearing retirement has an average of only $135,000 in their combined retirement accounts according to the Federal Reserve Survey of Consumer Finances. That will provide at most $600 per month income. Not even enough money to cover groceries, let alone health care, heating, transportation, and other necessities.
- As many as 60% of U.S. households are at risk of not having enough money to make ends meet in retirement—*even* if they cut back spending to just 75% of pre-retirement levels (2018 Center for Retirement Research study titled *How Much Income Do Retirees Actually Have?*).
- The average 65-year-old will **outlive their savings by almost a decade**, according to a June 2019 White Paper by the World Economic Forum *[Investing in (and for) our Future]*.

And those folks are the fortunate ones. Nearly half (48%) of all pre-retirees aged 55 and over have *zero* savings of *any* kind according to a March 2019 report from the U.S. Government Accountability

Office. Somebody or other really hit it on the head when he observed, "*I have enough money to live comfortably for the rest of my life—if I die by next Tuesday!*"

"But I'm Doing Better Than That"

Maybe these statistics don't reflect you. Maybe you've been serious and committed to planning for retirement. Good for you! On average, the top 10% of wage earners have saved about two years' worth of income.[3] Maybe you've done well and have put together $1 million or more for retirement—woohoo! Let's ignore the uncertainty of the market for a minute and pretend that money will remain safe and sound until you retire and throughout your retirement (and if you close your eyes, maybe the pixies will come and clean your house, pay your bills and mow the lawn as well).

Have you calculated how many years your retirement money will have to last you? Remember when I mentioned that your life in retirement will likely last much longer than you thought? A 65-year-old man today can expect to live until he's 84.3 on average and a 65-year-old woman can expect to live until 86.7 on average. One out of four 65-year-olds today will live past 90. One out of 10 will even live past 95, according to the Social Security Administration. Which means you *really* need to plan on your money lasting you until *at least* age 95 or 100 to be safe, just in case you're one of the lucky ones. And if you're well-educated or affluent, statistics show that you'll live even longer than the averages.

Yet many financial planners use age 85 when calculating how much money you'll need in retirement. (They probably assume you plan on moving in with your grandchildren and eating Top Ramen for breakfast, lunch, and dinner after that age.)

And let's say that you're calculating what you'll be able to spend using the "4% rule," which for years was the recommended withdrawal rate which said that retirees could take 4% out of their retirement accounts each year. Unfortunately, in recent years, the 4% rule has been found to give you *only a 50% probability* of not running out of money over 30 years! (I don't know about you, but I wouldn't be too eager to get on a plane that had only a 50% chance of landing safely!)

The *current* recommended annual withdrawal rate is *just 2.8%*—which gives you a 90% probability of having your money last for 30 years.[4] (Not perfect, but a lot better odds, right?) Withdrawing any more than 2.8% means increasing the odds that you will outlive your money. So let's take a closer look at what a withdrawal rate of 2.8% looks like. A $1 million nest egg would provide you only $28,000 a year or $2,333/month. A $500,000 nest egg would give you $14,000 a year or $1,166/month. And if you have $200,000 saved (which is almost 50% more than the average household), you could withdraw $5,600 per year or *just $467 per month*. Think about it: When you hit retirement, what kind of lifestyle do you think you'll have on $5,600, $14,000, or $28,000 per year? Does that even cover basic expenses? Will you need a greeter job at Wal-Mart—grinning at strangers for $8.47 per hour—to get by?

And here's the scary part: That money will *have to* cover more than just basic expenses. Here's why...

Healthcare Costs Not Covered by Medicare in Retirement

According to a Fidelity study, a 65-year-old couple retiring now will need $275,000 for out-of-pocket health care expenses not covered by Medicare. And at least 70% of people over age 65 will require long-term care, with more than 40% needing nursing home care at some point.[5] If you or your spouse require a stay in a nursing home, the average cost for a typical nursing home stay is about $250,000![6] And Medicare does *not* cover these expenses either.

Translation: The typical retired couple will likely need $500,000 or more *just* to cover their medical costs—and that's almost *four times more* than the typical couple approaching retirement has saved! Like I said, your retirement will likely cost far more than you planned for.

The typical retired couple will likely need $500,000 or more just to cover their medical costs.

Okay, but say you are the epitome of health. Dr. Oz calls you for advice on diet, and you plan to compete in the Iron Man when you're 89. Your plan is: healthy > healthy > healthy > dead. Sounds like a good plan, but there are still a few things that will eat away at your precious retirement funds that you can't avoid like ...

Inflation Takes Its Cut

We've experienced historically low inflation rates in recent years. The inflation rate was 1.9% for the year 2018, according to the U.S. Labor Department. So, it's easy to forget inflation has been a lot higher—in some years 10% or more. But even low rates of inflation eat away at the value of your retirement savings.

Scary fact: If inflation averages *just 3%* per year, it will swallow *more than $117,000* of the average Social Security benefit over 20 years, according to the LIMRA Secure Retirement Institute!

And who knows where inflation is headed. In the 100 years from 1913 – 2013, inflation averaged 3.22% a year, so many financial planners use a 3% figure when making projections. It doesn't sound like much, but a 3% annual inflation will deplete the purchasing power of your dollars by *more than half* over 25 years! In other words, whatever your cost of living is right now, you need to *double it* when projecting down the road.

How Much Money Do You Really Need in Retirement?

One guideline that is often cited is the "Rule of 25." The Rule of 25 says you should multiply your total annual expenses by 25 to determine how much you'll need to have saved by the time you retire. (Please note that I said "saved," not plunked down in the Wall Street Casino!) So, if you plan to spend $50,000 per year in retirement, you'll need to save $1.25 million. To have $100,000 per year to spend, you'll need $2.5 million, and if you want to live on $150,000 a year, you'll need $3.75 million saved. If your number is $250,000 a year, you need $6.25 million. (Not to assume, but I'm guessing your retirement fund isn't there yet.)

How many times your annual expenses have *you* saved? Are you confident that your retirement nest-egg will give you the freedom to enjoy retirement on *your* terms, without constant financial stress? Will you be able to travel? Spend more time with family and friends? Pursue your hobbies, develop your talents, do volunteer work—or live out whatever dreams you've had for your retirement?

According to a new study by the Stanford Center on Longevity, people need to save between 10% and 17% of their income if they plan to retire at 65 *even* if they start at age 25, but the vast majority are putting away only 6-8% of their income. That's only *half* of what they should be saving. What percent of your household income are you saving? It's important to be brutally honest with yourself because a shortfall of the magnitude most Americans will experience means more than just not being able to live the retirement lifestyle you dreamed of. It may mean...

- Being forced to choose between putting food on the table or getting the medical care you need
- Not being able to afford to pay for heating and air conditioning
- Having to rely on the charity of your children
- Foregoing travel and even life's little luxuries (like cable TV or your cell phone)

I doubt you worked hard all your life so that you can scrimp and struggle just to get by in retirement.

Couldn't You Just Retire Later?

When faced with the dismal statistics about retirement, many people simply try to accept the fact that they won't be able to retire when they had planned. "Hey, I enjoy my career, or at least I'm okay with it. I'll just keep working for a few more years—or forever." Unfortunately, according to the Employee Benefit Research Institute, **almost half of all retirees are forced out of work earlier than they planned** due to layoffs, poor health, or the need to take care of a loved one. Working longer may not be a backup plan you can count on, even if you're okay with a job where you ask, "And would you like fries with that?" a hundred times a day.

Okay, even I'm getting a headache thinking about all this. But I want to tell you that you *can* take charge of your financial well-being in retirement. You *can* take back control of your finances and your retirement security by simply avoiding these five wealth-killing traps of conventional retirement plans:

1. They are **totally unpredictable,** so you have *no idea* what you'll actually end up with for your retirement.
2. You have **little to no control** over them.

3. Your money in conventional plans is in prison, giving you **little to no access**.
4. The ultimate **tax consequences** are frightening—and if you make $70,000 per year or more, the IRS has slapped a giant target on your back as I'll explain soon.
5. And last (but unfortunately not least), the **fees and expenses** of 401(k)s, IRAs and Roth plans will erode your retirement fund by 25-50%.

Grab a couple of aspirin if you need to and let's get educated about these five traps. But first, I'm going to briefly introduce an option that can be your saving grace. It's one that you probably don't know about—or that you have many misconceptions about. But as you'll soon discover, this option has NONE of the traps of conventional plans.

CHAPTER TWO

You Can Bank On Yourself

"Just cuz you're following a well-marked trail doesn't mean that whoever made it knew where they were goin'.

—TEXAS BIX BENDER

LET ME ask you, are you willing to see things differently? Are you willing to absorb the stats, validate the research, do your homework, and see if maybe the conventional financial wisdom you've followed is flawed? Are you willing to entertain the possibility that there might be a solid, time-tested strategy that few financial gurus will acknowledge but that hundreds of thousands of people like you are using successfully? (I was willing, and so now I'm one of those hundreds of thousands!)

I've Been There and Done That, Too

I'm guessing that my story isn't much different than yours. I worked hard and, though I can't say I was always perfect in handling my money, I knew I needed to prepare for retirement. After I met my husband Larry, we started investing in various financial products and strategies. We read the literature and listened to the "experts" but somehow we *never* came close to getting the returns we were told we should be able to get.

At one point, we figured the problem must be us. Maybe we just didn't have the Midas touch when it came to investing. So we ultimately ended up hiring three extremely well-paid (by us) experts—and all three of them *lost* us money during one of the longest-running bull markets in history! Apparently, none of those three had "the touch" either!

But we didn't give up and start stuffing our retirement savings into a mattress. I was coaching thousands of financial advisors on how to build their businesses, so I had access to a huge number of financial vehicles. I burned the midnight oil for years investigating *more than 450* different financial products, strategies, and vehicles. In the end, only a few passed my due diligence tests—and when we implemented them, even those turned out to be disappointments.

Finally, one of my financial advisor clients said, "Pamela, have you ever heard about this?" *This* turned out to be a little-known super-charged version of a financial asset that's increased in value every single year for more than 160 years: **dividend-paying whole life insurance.**

Okay, so now you may be ready to throw this book in the trash! But hold on. Don't tune me out, because this is *nothing* like the whole life insurance policies Suze Orman, Dave Ramsey, and most financial advisors love to hate.

Properly structured, the high cash value, dividend-paying whole life insurance policies I'll show you grow cash value *significantly faster* than the ones most financial advisors talk about, especially in the early years. They pay the advisor or insurance agent *50-70% less commission.* And you can use them as a powerful financial-management tool right from the start to reach your short term and long-term financial goals and dreams—without taking *any* unnecessary risks.

In fact, remember the Father of the 401(k), Ted Benna, who called his creation a "monster"? Benna recently revealed that he now puts most of his money in—yep, you caught the clue—**high cash-value dividend-paying whole life insurance.**

I'll give you an overview of how it all works in this chapter. If you want to go deeper, I've written two *New York Times* bestsellers about it. The most recent and most comprehensive one is called *The Bank On Yourself Revolution: Fire Your Banker, Bypass Wall Street, and Take Control of Your Own Financial Future.*

Folks who've joined the Bank On Yourself "revolution" aren't crazy radicals or wide-eyed optimists looking for a miracle to save them. They are just folks of all ages and all income levels who became tired of doing "all the right things" financially yet still had to worry about when the next market crash would scuttle their best-laid plans. They simply decided that enough was enough and they stopped acting like lemmings, putting all their money into financial vehicles that they couldn't predict or count on.

They chose to take control of their financial futures.

They put less money into their 401(k)s and IRAs, and some stopped funding them altogether. They pulled back on their mutual funds and stocks and bonds. They stopped letting the capriciousness of Wall Street and the seductive advice of financial "gurus" threaten their future financial wellbeing.

Instead, they built a solid financial foundation. These folks opted for a high-performing version of a financial vehicle that has survived and thrived every single year for more than 160 years, through *every* recession, boom, and bust, *including the Great Depression*. Because they did so, these folks could now move forward without the stress, worry, and uncertainty they had lived with in the past.

Hundreds of thousands of people who have embraced the Bank On Yourself method have seen their money grow safely and predictably *every* single year—even when the markets are tumbling. They can finally get a good night's sleep knowing:

- Their policies don't skip a beat when the stock and real estate markets crash.
- They don't gamble on Wall Street to accumulate a sizable nest egg. They don't have to worry about when the next crash might come and wipe out their life savings again.
- They can tell banks and finance and credit card companies to go take a hike and have access to the money they need, whenever and for whatever they need it, without begging for it and without penalties or delays.
- They don't need to depend on their employer or the government for their financial security.
- They don't have to worry about nasty surprises in fees and taxes when they want to access their retirement funds.

Bank On Yourself isn't a get-rich-quick scheme, and it does require some patience. But the rewards for that patience are substantial.

I wish I could say I'm the genius who invented this strategy, but I can't. It had started way before I learned about the financial tool and concept I call "Bank On Yourself." And I decided to call it Bank On Yourself because it lets people free themselves from economic slavery and move toward freedom and economic sanity. It allows them to stop depending on the government, Wall Street, banks, and finance companies for their financial needs and security. Bank On Yourself folks *bank on themselves* by using their own good judgment and their own good sense to keep their families financially secure, rather than relying on the mercy of faceless institutions.

What amazed me then—and amazes me still—is how few people were aware of this tool and how many myths and misconceptions there are about it. It became my mission to help educate others about Bank On Yourself, so they too could take back control.

How Are Bank On Yourself-Type Policies Different Than Other Whole Life Policies?

If you have a knee-jerk negative reaction to whole life insurance, you're not alone. Celebrity financial gurus (and probably your own financial advisor) have told you to avoid whole life insurance at all costs. But the high cash-value, low-commission, dividend-paying whole life insurance life policies used for the Bank On Yourself method are *dramatically different* from run-of-the-mill whole life policies. Financial advisors' objections to whole life simply don't apply to Bank On Yourself-type policies. Here are just four of those objections and why they don't apply to Bank On Yourself policies:

1. Financial pundits claim that the money you can access in the plan—your cash value—grows much too slowly in a whole life policy. They say that you typically won't have any cash value at all in the first couple of years.

This is true for some whole life policies. However, a Bank On Yourself-type high cash-value dividend-paying whole life insurance policy incorporates little-known riders or options that *dramatically accelerate* the growth of your money in the policy, especially in the early years. Adding these riders, or options, allows you to use your policy as a powerful financial management tool from day one.

2. Celebrity financial gurus say one reason for the slow growth in cash value in a traditional whole life policy is the high commissions paid to the insurance advisors who sell them. Again, true for some other policies. But when a qualified advisor structures a Bank On Yourself-type high cash-value dividend-paying whole life insurance policy for you, they receive *50-70% less commission* because much of your premium is directed into the riders that make your cash value grow significantly faster.

Unfortunately, many financial advisors and insurance agents aren't willing to take a 50% or more pay cut. They will steer you towards a product or strategy that's more profitable to them. People were having such a hard time finding an advisor willing to take a big cut in commission and who truly understood how to structure these policies correctly, that it led to the creation of a program to train and vet advisors on the Bank On Yourself concept. The Bank On Yourself Authorized Advisor training program is sponsored by a separate company (in which I have no ownership) chosen for its outstanding history in training advisors to help their clients reach their financial goals through the use of guaranteed permanent life insurance and annuities. Admissions requirements to this program are high, and only one out of every 20 who apply are accepted into the program.

Today, there are 200 Bank On Yourself Authorized Advisors in the U.S. and Canada who have this advanced training in the concept and the proper way to structure policies to your benefit. To get a referral to one of these Advisors who can structure your policy to maximize your cash value and who know which companies have the best policies for this strategy, go to **www.BankOnYourself.com/free-analysis**.

3. Many financial experts and advisors only discuss whole life policies in which the death benefit stays level for the life of the policy. But the fact is that level death benefit policies have become rare in the last couple decades.

In a dividend-paying whole life insurance policy, dividends you receive can be left in the policy to purchase additional coverage while at the same time growing your cash value in the most efficient way possible. A Bank On Yourself-type policy incorporates two riders or options that result in a much larger cash value *and* death benefit over time than a traditional whole life policy. To learn more about how this works, go to **www.BankOnYourself.com/design.**

4. The financial experts often complain that the insurance company "only pays you the death benefit and keeps your cash value" when the policy owner dies. Really? Then how do you explain this: In one of my policy statements posted at **www.BankOnYourself.com/policy-statement**, you can see that if I'd died on the date the statement was issued, my family would have received a check for $381,776, which is a few thousand dollars *more* than the original $250,000 death benefit *plus* the then-current total cash value ($128,361) *combined*.

It's amazing to me that so many financial advisors hold whole life insurance to a *totally different* (and higher) standard than any other financial vehicle. For example, if you have $100,000 of equity in your home and you sell it for $250,000, do you expect to end up receiving *both* amounts, for a total of $350,000? Of course not.

However, as I've just shown you, a Bank On Yourself-type policy can even deliver that advantage!

Dividend-Paying Whole Life Insurance as a Safe Wealth-Building Vehicle

When we think of saving, typically we think of a bank savings account or a CD or a money market account, not whole life insurance. But as economist Jesús Huerta de Soto noted in his book *Money, Bank Credit and Economic Cycles*:

> "The institution of life insurance ... is based on a series of technical, actuarial, financial and juridical principles of business behavior which have enabled it to perform its mission perfectly and survive economic crises and recessions which other institutions, especially banking, have been unable to overcome. Therefore the high 'financial death rate' of banks, which systematically suspend payments and fail without the support of the central bank, has historically contrasted with the health and technical solvency of life insurance companies. (In the last two hundred years, a negligible number of life insurance companies have disappeared due to financial difficulties.)."

With Bank On Yourself-type policies, you receive a guaranteed and predictable cash value increase *every* single year—in both good times and bad. And that's the *worst* case scenario. In addition, you have the potential to receive dividends. While not guaranteed, the companies preferred by Bank On Yourself Authorized Advisors have *paid dividends every year for more than 100 years*, including during the Great Depression.

These policies are designed so that the growth gets better every year—which gives you some built-in protection against inflation. Plus your premium is guaranteed to *never* increase.

But what about that old adage that you should just "buy term and invest the difference"? Well, that might seem to be a good strategy except that, as David Babbel, Emeritus Professor at The Wharton School notes, "People don't buy term insurance and invest the difference. They most likely rent the term, lapse it, and spend the difference."

For most of us, the whole life insurance scorned by financial pundits actually proves to be a lot safer and smarter—*if* you pick the right policy. Be warned: Not all cash-value life insurance policies are created equal. In fact, some of them, such as universal and indexed universal life, can be downright dangerous to your financial health. For example, over the last few years, Indexed Universal Life (IUL) has been the "hot" life insurance product making the rounds. If someone tries to sell you one of these policies, I urge you to read "*7 Reasons to Be Wary of Indexed Universal Life*" at **www.BankOnYourself.com/be-wary.**

These relatively new products are designed to sound like a sexy, can't-lose alternative to the stock market, but they do not give you the same guarantees whole life insurance gives. Lawsuits have been filed against companies that sell these products, and you can expect more over time. Do your own due diligence and don't jump from the frying pan into the fire. No other form of permanent or cash value life insurance comes with as many guarantees as whole life insurance.

No other form of permanent or cash value life insurance comes with as many guarantees as whole life insurance.

"How Can I Be Sure the Companies That Issue These Whole Life Policies Will Deliver on Their Promises?"

The companies recommended by Bank On Yourself Authorized Advisors are among the financially strongest life insurance groups in the country. In essence, they're owned by the policy owners, which means these companies *focus on the long-term best interests of the policy owners (you!) rather than the short-term demands of Wall Street.*

Here's the difference between dividend-paying whole life insurance policies as a wealth-building vehicle and most other products and strategies the financial gurus favor: On the freeway, can you spot the difference between a teenager putting daddy's hot sports car through its paces, and a young suburban mom in her minivan taking two kids to soccer practice with a toddler buckled in a car seat? One driver is trying to get somewhere fast, while the other is getting to her destination while doing everything possible to protect those who are near and dear to her. If you understand that difference, you'll understand the difference between the Wall Street Casino and the life insurance industry.

While guarantees are based on the claims-paying ability of the insurers, many people don't realize that life insurance companies are strictly regulated and enjoy a four-layer safety net:

1. They're audited regularly by the state insurance commissioner's office (sometimes by *dozens* of different states) to ensure they maintain sufficient reserves to pay future claims and that they are on solid financial ground.
2. If a company gets into financial difficulty, the state insurance commissioner's office can take over and run the company in the interests of policyholders. (Historically, a failed insurer's business is then taken over by another company, according to the National Organization of Life and Health Insurance Guaranty Associations.)
3. Most insurance companies are audited regularly by several independent rating companies.
4. Additional policy owner protections are available on a state-by-state basis. For example, in one annual policy statement I received, there was a notice regarding the various protections provided by the Insurance Guaranty Association of New Mexico, the state where I live.

In addition to these layers of protection, life insurance companies (especially those owned by their policyowners) are simply run *differently*. Remember that mom driving the minivan versus the kid in the hot sports car? These companies aren't trying to be flashy or grab short-term profits wherever they can. Their mission is to get you and your family to your destination safely.

More Facts of Life (Insurance)

- **Meets safe capital requirements:** Banks are legally required to have a foundation of very safe liquid assets, known as Tier 1 capital. Life insurance is considered to be so safe that bank regulators allow banks to use life insurance policies to meet their Tier 1 capital requirements. In fact, according to the most recent data available provided by Equias Alliance, the nation's banks owned guaranteed, permanent life insurance with a surrender value of approximately $166 billion.

- **Diversified low-risk investments:** In the companies recommended by Bank On Yourself Authorized Advisors, the bulk of their portfolios is invested in investment-grade fixed-income assets. Their bond portfolios are highly diversified across many industries and companies, and typically, no investment represents more than 2% of assets. Less than 2% is usually invested in U.S. Treasury or other government debt.

Due to their financial strength and reserves, these companies have the ability to hold on to any assets that may decline in value for many years until those assets recover.

- **Source of capital, even in tough times:** Life insurance cash values serve as a source of available capital to individuals, families, and businesses— even when credit is difficult to obtain. According to the latest data available, policyholders had $129 billion in life insurance policy loans outstanding, and they're using this money for *any* purpose they choose with *no* restrictions whatsoever.

- **Bedrock of our grandparents' savings plans:** Back in 1900, *half* of all Americans' savings was held in life insurance and annuities. And fully *one-third of families* owned whole life insurance policies in 1950.

- **Help great businesses succeed:** Many famous people have used life insurance policy loans to start or grow their businesses. Following the 1929 stock market crash, retailer J. C. Penney borrowed against his life insurance policies to help meet the company payroll and keep the doors open.

Walt Disney borrowed from his life insurance policy in 1953 to help fund Disneyland when the Disney Board rejected the concept saying it was a crazy idea that would never be profitable. Ray Kroc of McDonald's had constant cash flow problems in the beginning, so he borrowed from his policies to cover salaries and to pay for the Ronald McDonald advertising campaign. (Can you imagine a world without those Golden Arches everywhere?)

Doris Christopher started the Pampered Chef with $3,000 she borrowed from her life insurance policy and ended up selling the company to Warren Buffett for a reported $1.5 billion. And Max and Verda Foster borrowed $1,000 against their life insurance policy to buy an eighty-acre farm near Modesto, CA to begin Foster Farms.

In 2009, when banks had their money on lock-down, I was able to get my hands on $500,000 for a business opportunity, and it was in my checking account within a week—*no questions asked*—thanks to the ability to borrow against my whole life insurance policies!

"But Won't I Miss Out When the Market is Hot?"

If you're into horror movies and high-speed no-hands roller coaster rides when it comes to your finances, Bank On Yourself may not be for you. To some people, the safe and predictable growth of Bank On Yourself just isn't very sexy. (Then again to folks like me, the financial peace of mind it brings is an unparalleled aphrodisiac!)

When you Bank On Yourself, you may feel left out when your friends start bragging about the killing they're making in the latest hot investment—real estate, tech or oil stocks, commodities, cryptocurrency, gold, or ostrich farms. You might miss out on the thrill of chasing returns and trying to anticipate the exact perfect timing to buy or sell that juicy investment. Bank On Yourself is all about building a solid financial foundation and a secure future—no matter *what's* happening in the markets or the economy. It's the minivan, not the sports car! You're not going to experience thrilling spikes—but you're also not going to get hit with those unpredictable, heart-stopping losses that inevitably follow!

And the growth of your money in a Bank On Yourself policy is not just "on paper" the way investments are. Your friend who's bragging about how much money he's making in the stock market? In reality, he hasn't made *a dime* until he actually *sells* his investments and (hopefully!) locks in his profits. That neighbor who's so excited that her rental property has appreciated by 20%? Until she sells it, she hasn't made squat. And those poor investors who bought Bitcoin? They watched it skyrocket 30-fold over 2 1/2 years, only to watch it flame out like a cheap sparkler on the 4th of July. As I write this, Bitcoin's value is rising again, but will it end up being another fake-out for investors? Those paper profits may make for a good temporary high, but they aren't real until they are *realized*.

...the growth of your money in a Bank On Yourself policy is not just "on paper" the way investments are.

In contrast, when you look at the annual statement for your Bank On Yourself policy or check your policy values online, the numbers you see represent *real money*, not just paper wealth. Both your principle *and* growth are **locked in**. They don't go backward even in a market crash.

If you need or want that occasional investment high, keep in mind that Bank On Yourself isn't an either/or proposition. When you own a Bank On Yourself-type policy, and you want to take advantage of an investment opportunity that comes up, you can do it by borrowing against the equity (cash value) from your policy. You'll continue to get the *same* guaranteed annual increase, *plus* the same dividends on the money you borrowed, which means your money can be working for you in two places at once *if* your policy is from one of the companies that offer this feature. (However, if your investment tanks and you can't pay back the loan, or at least its interest, your policy might lapse which could result in an income tax liability on any gains. So be cautious about using your *safe* money for *risky* investments!)

Caution: Not all companies offer a whole life policy with the feature that pays you the exact same dividends even on the money you borrowed. That's why we always recommend that you work with a Bank On Yourself Authorized Advisor who knows how to properly structure your policy for maximum growth and knows which companies offer the policies that let you take full advantage of this concept.

Only a handful of companies offer policies that have *all* the features needed to maximize the Bank On Yourself concept. To get a referral to a qualified Bank On Yourself Advisor who knows which companies have the best policies, is willing to take a lower commission, and who knows how to structure your policy to maximize your growth, go to **www.BankOnYourself.com/free-analysis.**

A key point is that having money safe and liquid in a Bank On Yourself-type policy gives you *more* options, not fewer.

I could give you tons more detail about Bank On Yourself, but I promised to keep this book brief.

Now that you have an overview, let's get back to those five wealth-killing retirement plan traps you want to avoid—unpredictability, little or no control, lack of access to your money, the future tax time bomb, and high fees and expenses—and let's compare Bank On Yourself-type high cash value dividend-paying whole life policies to conventional retirement plans.

CHAPTER THREE:

Retirement Plan Trap #1: Unpredictability

"The main purpose of the stock market is to make fools of as many men as possible."

—BERNARD BARUCH, Financier

HERE'S THE million-dollar question: Is your money for retirement safe, guaranteed to grow, and protected from market volatility? If your retirement fund is in a conventional plan, unless you've parked your cash in a CD, money market account, or fixed annuity (options that not all plans offer), the answer is "Absolutely Not!"

Is your money for retirement safe, guaranteed to grow, and protected from market volatility?

Before 1978, speculating in stocks was a pastime of the wealthy. Today, thanks to the explosive growth of 401(k) plans, mutual funds, and the Internet, the typical working person has bet his financial future on a roll of the dice in the Wall Street Casino.

Despite the fact that we *can't afford to lose* the money we'll need for retirement, we've been told that the best way to grow a substantial nest egg is to risk our money in the market, especially through tax-deferred, government-approved market-based retirement accounts like 401(k)s, 403(b)s, IRAs, SEP-IRAs, and Keogh Plans.

Here's the deal: If your money is invested in the market, you could lose some or even all of it—and you never know ***when*** that might happen! No one can tell you what the market will be doing on a certain day or in a certain year, so you have no way of predicting what the value of your plan will be when you're ready to tap into it.

The Problem with Target Date Funds (TDFs)

If you have a 401(k), it's very possible that your money is in a Target Date Fund (TDF), *even if you didn't authorize or request it!* Here's why that should concern you:

TDFs are mutual funds that invest in a mix of assets, shifting from higher-risk to lower-risk investments as participants approach their target retirement date. Based on an analysis from Fidelity Investments, *MarketWatch* reported that, as of 2018, *more than half of all 401(k) accounts had fully 100% of their assets in TDFs.* More than 30% of all assets of all 401(k)s are in TDFs. Slightly more than 50% of all 401(k) savers and 62% of savers in 403(b) plans have 100% of their assets in TDFs. The report also said that 98% of all employers use TDFs, 90% of which have it as the default option for their employees (which means your employer automatically puts your money in this option unless you specifically tell them otherwise).

Under provisions of the Pension Protection Act of 2006, eligible workers can be automatically enrolled in 401(k) plans unless they explicitly choose to opt out of participation, and TDFs have emerged as by far the most popular *default investment*—the one your employer automatically chooses *for* you. And, according to Towers Watson, a global financial consulting firm, 90% (!) of all new hires let their plan administrator choose where their money will be invested for them.

There are many problems with TDFs. One of them is, as Dennis Nolte, VP of Seacoast investment Services, noted, "These plans treat everyone as if they have the same risk tolerance and income needs in retirement, and can tolerate the volatility before the 'target year' is reached."

Still, it seems to make good sense in theory. Take more risks when you're young and dial back the risk as you get older. But in practice, it's been a disaster! A report from the federal government's General Accountability Office (GAO) revealed that during the last recession, investors in the largest TDF funds *lost as much as 31% of their money.* That 31% loss is outrageous, especially considering that the Dow Jones Industrial Average lost only 1.61% during that very same time period!

It gets worse. The GAO report also states, "As a result of the severe financial market turbulence of 2008, some TDFs designed for participants [planning to retire in just two years] lost considerable value, just over 40% in one case. Further, according to some experts, many participants were unaware of the risks associated with these investments and that such losses were possible so close to the retirement date."

...some TDFs designed for participants [planning to retire in just two years] lost considerable value, just over 40% in one case.

Can you imagine being just *months* from retirement, only to see your nest egg take a 40% hit? Would you be stunned? Devastated?

What if another major market crash happens right before you plan to retire? What makes you think TDFs will perform any better the next time the market tanks? By the way, when your employer follows the law and *automatically* puts your money into TDFs, you have no recourse if your plan loses a bundle because the Pension Protection Act of 2006 gave your employer protection from liability. They take your money, make poor decisions with it, then it's, "Sorry, Charlie. Better luck next time!"

In fact, a study from the Center for Retirement Research at Boston College found that plan administrators routinely make poor decisions, choosing mutual funds that *lag comparable indexes.* Just like the rest of us humans, they routinely chase returns. About the best thing the study said was that, even though employers choose funds that lag the indexes, at least their choices were better than randomly selected funds. (Translation: Their choices were marginally better than rolling the dice or a monkey throwing darts.)

Bad for Your Health as Well as Your Wealth

Even if your fund manager is relatively competent, the stock market is volatile and capricious. And it turns out, this unpredictability isn't just dangerous to your retirement security. Studies show that even relatively small stock market declines are linked to *early death, illness, and fatal car accidents!* In fact, if you have even 10% of your wealth in the stock market and experience only a 10% loss, your risk of dying early, or having a physical health problem, like high blood pressure, or a mental health problem, such as depression, increases significantly.

According to a recent study published in the American Economic Journal, when the market drops 10%, out of 100 retirees with funds in the market, one additional person will die and 2.5 more will develop health problems over the following two years. Another study that examined patient records for every hospital in California over nearly three decades found that, when the market fell nearly 25%, "hospital admissions spiked over 5%" *immediately.*

Studies show that even relatively small stock market declines are linked to early death, illness, and fatal car accidents!

Life is stressful enough on its own. Do we really need to add the stress of worrying about what might happen to the money we've worked so hard to earn?

Bank On Yourself Lets You Sleep at Night

The money you put into your Bank On Yourself-type policy and the growth you receive on it are simply *not going to disappear.* You're not going to open your statement to find that 40% or more of the money you'll need for retirement evaporated because the latest Ponzi scheme from hot-shot investment bankers toppled the market.

Nope. The money you put in remains *secure* due to all the protections and conservative business practices built into the DNA of the life insurance industry. The guaranteed growth of your money in a Bank On Yourself policy is *predictable,* not some guesstimate based on the phase of the moon or the whims of Wall Street. And you'll know up front exactly how much growth that will be *without* the dozens of disclaimers in flea-sized font of other financial vehicles. On top of that, you have the potential for dividends. Dividends are *not* guaranteed, but they have been paid *every single year* for more than 100 years by the companies recommended by Bank On Yourself Authorized Advisors. Their track record is so good because life insurance companies are masters at under-promising and over-delivering—unlike the greedy pit bosses in the Wall Street casino.

A 2% TOTAL Return During the Bull Market?

Bank On Yourself "kept us safe and sane during the stock market crash," reported Debbie Wilder. "We started our first four Bank On Yourself policies eleven years ago—one for me, one for my husband, and one each for our two kids. When we were maxing out our 401(k) s and IRAs, we were only up 2% total over a 14-year period which included the bull market of the 1990s! Our Bank On Yourself policies never go backward, and the increases are guaranteed and predictable. We're excited to watch our nest egg grow."

As people get older, they are typically advised to take less risk with their money to avoid losing significant amounts right before or during retirement. Following the conventional wisdom, that means accepting very low growth in exchange for more stability.

But the Bank On Yourself strategy turns that entire notion upside down. Your cash value is *guaranteed* to grow by a larger dollar amount each year— and it does so ***without your taking on more risk***. In a Bank On Yourself-type whole life policy, the growth is greatest at the time people usually need it most—in retirement.

CHAPTER FOUR:

Retirement Plan Trap #2: You Have Little or No Control

"Men, it has been well said, think in herds; it will be seen that they go mad in herds, while they only recover their senses slowly, one by one."

—CHARLES MACKAY, Scottish journalist

I DON'T CONSIDER myself a control freak (though my husband might tell a different story!). But I think all of us should have some control over our *own money*, right? Yet when you put money into a conventional retirement plan, it's like burying it in a time capsule that you can't open for 20 to 30 years—or more!

It's Like Putting Your Money in Prison

When you put your money in a government-sponsored retirement account, it's like you've sent it to a maximum-security prison. Someone else calls the shots now and you barely get visitation rights! In most of these plans, the prison wardens (the government and your company) will determine:

1. *How much* you may put in your plan
2. What you *can and cannot invest in*
3. *If* you can borrow from your plan, *how much* you can borrow as well as *when and how* you *must* pay it back
4. *How long* you *must* wait before you can access your money
5. When you *must* start taking out your money and how much you *must* withdraw (and pay taxes on)

Penalties for running afoul of these regulations are extremely costly.

Withdrawal rules are particularly restrictive: You'll pay *penalties* for taking most distributions before you're 59½, and you're *forced* to start taking distributions in your early 70s—whether or not you want to or need to. A big complaint I hear today is from seniors who don't want to start withdrawing but are being forced to take Required Minimum Distributions (RMDs) from their retirement plans —and *that's pushing them into a higher tax bracket*. Why does the government do this? Because they can't afford to wait any longer to start collecting those taxes they let you defer all those years.

Roth plans don't have the Required Minimum Distributions requirement. However, a Roth plan still has restrictions about 1) *how much* you are allowed to put in each year, 2) *how soon* you may withdraw your earnings, and 3) *where* you can invest it.

No, Virginia, you do *not* control the money in your 401(k) or IRA, or any similar plan. The *government* has its tentacles all over it and can—and does!—change the rules any time they want! The prison warden has your money on lockdown, and while your money's in the slammer, he can arbitrarily impose any new restrictions or regulations he dreams up—and you have *no* recourse.

Here are two critical questions to ask about your current retirement accounts:

1. Can you put in as much as you want and take out what you want when and how you want it?
2. Do you have a say in what rules your employer and the government set regarding the money in your plan?

If, like most Americans, you followed conventional wisdom and have a conventional retirement plan, the answer to each of these questions is "no."

Are Self-Directed IRAs the Solution?

What about self-directed IRAs? People have the mistaken impression that self-directed means you don't have to operate within government controls and restrictions. Not so. You can determine what investments to place in the plan, but even that is within limits the government sets. A self-directed plan operates under the same rules and restrictions as a traditional IRA, and the government prohibits a myriad of transactions.

Plus now the Securities and Exchange Commission has gotten into the act. In fact, in August of 2018, the SEC's Office of Investor Education and Advocacy sent out an alert "to warn investors of risks associated with self-directed IRAs." Here are some excerpts from that frightening alert:

".... self-directed IRAs raise the risks including ***fraudulent schemes, high fees, and volatile performance*** *... may allow investors to invest retirement funds in 'alternate assets' such as real estate, promissory notes, tax lien certificates, and private placement securities ... assets may have unique risks that investors should consider ... Fraudsters may be more likely to exploit self-directed IRAs because custodians or trustees of these accounts may offer only limited protections."*

To paraphrase a quote from the movie Rounders, "If you can't spot the sucker in the room, it's you."

Rules and Regulations Can Be Changed Without Your Consent

Oh, and by the way, your company can change your 401(k) plan's rules and participation rates with little or no notice, throwing years of your careful planning into chaos. For example, at one point, IBM decided to no longer give employees their 401(k) match during each pay cycle. Instead, IBM decided to make one lump-sum payment to employee accounts on the *last day* of each year, December 31. Employees lost an entire year of growth on the match money—and if an employee is fired or quits just before the end of the year, he won't get *any* match for the year.

Is your company next in line to change or scale back its 401(k) plan?

Will the Government Take Over Your Retirement Account?

It's not widely publicized (because it *certainly* wouldn't be popular!), but the government frequently floats proposals to take more control over government-approved retirement accounts. For example, they've wanted to limit how much you can accumulate in your retirement account (and defer taxes on). Why? Because it could generate billions in current tax revenue and because some administrations have believed there should be a limit on how much money you can accumulate for retirement. Apparently, the government thinks it knows better than you do how much money is too much!

Government-approved retirement plans are an incredibly attractive target for government control and ownership. Why? For the same reason, notorious holdup man Willie Sutton gave when he was asked why he robbed banks: "That's where the money is!"

The government created and tracks these plans, so they know precisely where your money is and how much you have there.

YOU Control Your Money in a Bank On Yourself Policy

Unlike government-approved retirement plans, life insurance policies are private contracts. With a Bank On Yourself-type policy, the income you take out and the growth of the policy are generally not even reported to the IRS. Your privacy is protected. So when the government is looking to get its greedy little hands on more money, odds are they'll go for the lower hanging fruit in the retirement plans they sponsor and control.

In addition to being private, life insurance contracts are also "unilateral" contracts. This means the company can't change any aspects of your contract unless *you* agree to it. That's the law.

As a policy owner, *you* control the money that's accumulating in the policy. That's the way it works. You decide how much premium you'd like to pay into your policy. The upper limit is determined by your income, assets, and life insurance needs, not a government-imposed limitation. You can borrow against the cash value of your policy any time you want. You don't have to "qualify" or beg for a loan. And nothing in your policy contract requires you to pay a loan back on a certain schedule or face stiff penalties, collection calls and dings on your credit report.

When you hit retirement, *you* decide when and how you want to take your retirement income, without facing government restrictions or penalties for "early" withdrawals or waiting "too long." You won't pay penalties for taking "too little" each year, unlike the mandatory minimum annual withdrawal requirements in tax-deferred government-approved retirement plans.

CHAPTER FIVE

Retirement Plan Trap #3: Conventional Plans "Freeze" Your Money

"Refuse to be stampeded. Do your own thinking."

—B. C. FORBES, founder of Forbes magazine

HERE'S A key question: How quickly and easily can you get your hands on the money in your retirement account when you need or want it?

With 401(k)s, IRAs, and similar plans, you typically have to sell the investment that you were counting on for growth if you want to get your money out. If it's a bad time to sell, you're out of luck. You have to bite the bullet and take a loss. And if you need to withdraw money before age 59½, in most cases you'll pay a stiff penalty.

Some 401(k) plans allow you to borrow money from your account, but they don't make it easy. Taking a loan from your 401(k) at a typical company requires a 13-step approval process. And if your plan does permit borrowing, the government imposes strict and low limits on how much you can borrow, how long you can borrow it for, and how often and how large your loan repayments must be. If you lose your job or leave your company for any reason while you have a loan outstanding (and you haven't reached the magic age of 59½), *you're required to pay your loan back in full* ***with*** *interest by the due date of your next federal tax return*, or you'll have to pay income taxes on the money you borrowed *plus* a 10% penalty. So you've got less than four months to pay it all back if you get laid off or fired on December 31st!

Wait! Wasn't this *your* money in the first place? But when your money is in the government-controlled retirement plan penitentiary, you can't even get it out on parole without major hassles and penalties!

Some plans don't even allow workers to make any new contributions until they've paid off their loans. Others require workers to wait a set time before contributing again after taking a loan or withdrawal. If your employer matches contributions, you'd be taking a double hit.

Aside from the penalties and taxes you may end up owing when you borrow from your 401(k), one study reported in the New York Times calculated that a thirty-five-year-old with a $20,000 plan balance who takes out two loans in fifteen years ends up with *about $38,000 less* at age sixty-five than someone who never borrows, even if the loans are repaid without penalty. So why, when you do everything required to use *your own money*, do you still get dinged?

It's even worse if you default on your loan.

Maybe you think you're someone who would *never* default on a loan. Of course, no one *intends* to default on a loan. But Dr. Brigitte Madrian, a Harvard University economist, estimates that 15% of 401(k) loan balances go into default and at least 75% of workers who leave their jobs with a loan outstanding end up defaulting and getting stuck paying penalties and taxes.

Oh, and by the way, borrowing from your IRA is verboten. The plan custodian will report it to the IRS, and the value of your *entire* IRA immediately becomes taxable. *Even using your IRA as collateral for a loan triggers taxes.*

...at least 75% of workers who leave their jobs with a loan outstanding end up defaulting and getting stuck paying penalties and taxes.

Borrowing from your Roth plan or using it as collateral for a loan is also prohibited. At least with a Roth plan, you can withdraw the contributions you made to the plan without any penalties or taxes (because you fund a Roth plan with money you've already paid taxes on). However, if you withdraw your growth or earnings before you turn 59½ and before the account is 5 years old, that withdrawal *will* be subject to taxes and may be subject to penalties. Of course, any money you withdraw will no longer earn you any interest or investment income.

Bank On Yourself Gives Your Money a "Get Out of Jail Free" Card

Bank On Yourself gives you complete control over the equity (cash value) in your policy. You can take a loan against your equity whenever you want, for whatever you want, with **no** government restrictions. There are *no* penalties for early withdrawals, late withdrawals, or no withdrawals, unlike government-sponsored conventional plans. You can get to the money you need *when* you need it, become your own source of financing and fire your banker! And you can repay it on your *own* terms. You have complete control and flexibility.

Whenever I write about this feature of Bank On Yourself, I hear from literally *dozens* of people who had a desperate but legitimate need for cash, but they couldn't get what they needed out of their 401(k)!

With Bank On Yourself-type policies, you have full access to 85% or more of the cash value of your policy *beginning the very first month*, without selling your assets to do it. In fact—and this is one of the hardest things for people to grasp—if your policy is administered by one of the handful of companies that offer this feature, *when you borrow money, your policy can continue growing just as if you hadn't touched a dime of it.* To learn more about how policy loans work, check out our Consumer Guide to Life Insurance Loans at **www.BankOnYourself.com/policy-loans.**

Key Point: You can literally get your hands on the money you need from your Bank On Yourself-type policy within days. Here's the simple explanation of how that works. The money you borrow doesn't actually come from *your* policy. It comes out of the company's general fund because all the cash value of all the policies is pooled together. You're actually borrowing *against* your cash value, using your cash value and death benefit as collateral for the loan. So, the money you borrow can still grow as if you never touched it because it never left your policy!

Key Point: You can literally get your hands on the money you need from your Bank On Yourself-type policy within days.

There's *no one* telling you what you can and cannot use your money for or imposing stiff penalties if you don't follow their rules to the letter. It really *is* your money. As it should be!

No Permission Needed to Use Your Money

"I didn't want to have to ask for permission to use my money," remarked David Shelton, a healthcare V.P. in Texas. "I had very limited control of my money in my 401(k). I couldn't put in as much as I wanted, and I needed permission to borrow my own money if necessary. Bank On Yourself gives me control over my money. We're also using it to pay for our two sons' private school educations in one installment to take advantage of a discount."

CHAPTER SIX

Retirement Plan Trap #4: The Tax Man Cometh

"Anyone may arrange his affairs so that his taxes shall be as low as possible; he is not bound to choose that pattern which best pays the treasury."

—LEARNED HAND, American judge

LET'S CUT to the chase: Do you know what surprises the tax man has in store for you when you take money out of your conventional tax-deferred retirement plan? Let me answer that for you: No.

Most people look at their retirement plan balances and think it's all theirs. They tend to forget they'll owe the IRS taxes on *every* penny they've put in and *every* penny of growth that they've deferred all these years. Out of sight, out of mind. Is this a big deal? According to Boston College's Center for Retirement Research Director, Alicia Munnell, "It's a very big deal when people realize they only have *two-thirds* or *three-quarters* of what they thought they had [in their tax-deferred retirement account]."

With the exception of Roth plans, money you put in a government-sponsored retirement plan isn't taxed now. But it *will* be taxed later. The money you put into a tax-deferred retirement plan is money you haven't paid taxes on. Over time, you hope that money grows. Later, you'll pay tax on *everything* you withdraw from the plan—your contributions, any employer match you've received, *and* any growth you've gotten over the years (hopefully, your account *has* grown, right?).

It's a very big deal when people realize they only have *two-thirds* or *three-quarters* of what they thought they had [in their tax-deferred retirement account].

Conventional wisdom says you'll come out ahead by deferring taxes. After all, doesn't that mean your entire contribution can go to work for you immediately? Unfortunately, like many assumptions about personal finance, this simply isn't true. According to the Society of Actuaries, if tax rates remain the same, *"It doesn't make any difference whether the taxes are taken away from you at the beginning (before you put the money in a financial vehicle) or at the end (tax-deferred).* ***It's the same fraction of your money that is left to you.***"

Deferred taxes might sound good today, but it's like putting off a visit to the dentist. The problem will only get worse, and that's because as you've been trying to build your so-called "secure" nest egg through conventional plans, the deferred-taxes strategy has created massive financial *insecurity*. Look, I love little surprises from my husband. But surprises from the tax man are *never* warm and fuzzy.

When the tax man eventually comes calling, he won't ask you what your tax liability *would* have been if you'd been paying taxes all along. He'll tell you what your tax liability is *at the time the taxes are due*. If the tax rates get lower over the years, you might come out ahead.

However, most people, including most financial experts, believe tax rates will head *higher*, not lower, over the long term. And your retirement could last 20-30 years or more.

Are You Sitting on a Tax Time Bomb?

The reality is that you are probably sitting on a tax time bomb. Simply put, the government is going to need more money in years to come for several reasons. For example, let's look at the numbers impacting Social Security and Medicare.

Today there are 62 million Americans using Social Security and Medicare. By 2045, 140 million—more than *twice* as many—Baby Boomers and Gen X-ers will be over 65 and requiring Social Security and Medicare. Where do you think the money to pay for that will come from? Will the government get that money from the 75% of Americans who don't have much money—or the 25% who do?

What do you think it takes to be in the top 25% of American wage earners? If you made $69,007 or more in 2017, you're in the top 25%.[7] And if you made $118,400 or more in 2017, you're in the top 10% of all wage earners.[8]

As nice as it may sound to be in the top 10% or even the top 25%, it also means you've got a *giant target on your back* when the government is looking for more revenue to cover its obligations.

Social Security and Medicare's financial condition has *deteriorated* despite a long economic expansion. In fact, Social Security is already in a negative cash flow situation. What will happen to those funds in the next downturn? Could the government correct this situation by reducing benefits rather than raising taxes? Maybe. But that would just mean another negative hit to your retirement income in the form of lower benefits.

And what about the national debt? Washington has been spending like a drunken sailor and kicking the debt can down the road for *decades*. As of June 2019, the national debt had ballooned to over *$22.3 trillion*—which comes to *$871,258 for each family!* And it's still climbing. (For a painful wake-up call, check out USDebtClock.org)

When Washington is finally forced to fix the problem, higher taxes are inevitable. I've asked thousands of people what they think will happen to tax rates over the long term. Virtually all of them—including most experts—believe tax rates will *have to* go up. I'll bet you're in that camp too.

So if tax rates do go up (which seems highly likely) and you're successful in growing your nest egg, you'll only be paying *higher* taxes on a *bigger* number. Doesn't it make sense to pay your taxes *now* while the tax rates are at historic lows rather than stockpiling money that the IRS and government can tax any way they want to in the future?

And what if the government changes its mind about letting you defer taxes on your plan? A recent *Forbes* article reported that "the government lost $82.7 billion in potential revenue from 401(k) taxes as fiscal year 2016 came to a close" which makes your retirement account a tempting target for legislators who calculate they could bring in an additional $584 billion from government-sponsored retirement plans within four years. Will they do that? Who knows? But *you* have absolutely *no control* over whether they do or not, meaning that your carefully constructed financial "plan" is really just a crapshoot.

I get it. Paying taxes now, like going to the dentist now, isn't fun. But trusting that somehow, someway your tax bite will be lower in the future is a root canal waiting to happen.

...trusting that somehow, someway your tax bite will be lower in the future is a root canal waiting to happen.

You Can Minimize Your Lifetime Tax Bite

With a Bank On Yourself-type policy, it's possible to take a retirement income *without* taxes due under current tax law. This is accomplished through a combination of dividend withdrawals and loans against your cash value while making sure the policy doesn't terminate.

By building your retirement nest egg using the Bank On Yourself strategy, you get to enjoy several tax advantages. Of course, tax laws can change, but the following tax benefits have withstood the test of time:

1. You can take a retirement income with no taxes due. There are two types of Bank On Yourself-type policies. In the most common one, the tax treatment is similar to Roth plans but without the restrictions of a Roth plan. You put in dollars on which you have already paid income tax. You pay your taxes up front while you know what they are and eliminate any unpleasant surprises in the future. On the gains you have each year (and you *will* have gains—guaranteed!), there are *no* taxes to slow the growth of your money.

Then, similar to Roth plans, you can access your principal and growth with *no taxes due*. Here's how: Dividends you leave in your policy to be reinvested are not taxable, and dividends you withdraw from your policy are not taxed unless you exceed your cost basis (the premium you paid in). If you get close to having withdrawn your cost basis, you can switch to borrowing against your cash value, with no taxes due on policy loans as long as you don't let your policy lapse.

The other type of policy is what I call the Bank On Yourself for Seniors policy for folks up to age 85. It involves a single lump sum premium rather than ongoing premiums and has a different tax treatment. Gains are tax-deferred until you withdraw them. To learn more about this and see several examples of this strategy in action, go to **www.BankOnYourself.com/seniors.**

2. You can reduce the taxes you may have to pay on your Social Security benefits. Many people don't know that it's fairly common, even for middle-income folks, to pay taxes on Social Security benefits. Currently, if a couple makes over $32,000 (from retirement account withdrawals and certain other sources), 50% of their Social Security income gets taxed. If they make more than $44,000, up to 85% of their Social Security benefits are taxed. Doesn't it bother you that the government may require you to pay taxes on the money you get from Social Security—a system you paid your hard-earned money into for all those years? It's like double jeopardy!

However, the income you take in retirement from a Bank On Yourself policy is *not* included in the income totals the IRS uses to determine whether (or how much) your Social Security check is taxed. So you won't be penalized for being responsible and creating additional retirement income.

3. If you're a business owner, you can get extra tax breaks. Professionals and other business owners are increasingly using Bank On Yourself to become their own source of financing for business vehicles, equipment, office buildings, and more. When you finance business expenses this way, you can qualify for tax deductions for interest and depreciation. Plus this strategy lets you recapture the interest you'd otherwise pay to banks and other financial institutions and never see again. (See **www.BankOnYourself.com/business** for more on how business owners and professionals use the Bank On Yourself method.)

4. The death benefit, which is typically many times greater than your cash value, passes to your loved ones and favorite charities income tax-free. It avoids the expense and publicity of passing through probate, too.

John Goodson, the late co-founder and chairman of the faculty of the College of Estate Planning Attorneys noted, "*The idea of turning a life insurance policy into a more flexible Roth IRA substitute, when estates both large and small are involved, is a real winner. The Bank On Yourself strategy also enables setting up asset protection, stand-by emergency money, and tax and administrative savings. Bravo, bravissimo!"*

CHAPTER SEVEN

Retirement Plan Trap #5: Fees That Compound Against You

"The miracle of compounding returns is overwhelmed by the tyranny of compounding costs."

—JOHN BOGLE, creator of the first index mutual fund and founder of Vanguard

WE ALL know that when compound interest is working *for* you, it's a thing of beauty. But in traditional retirement plans, just like with deferred taxes, the compounding of fees works *against* you, and that's just plain ugly. It doesn't matter whether you win or lose in the stock market, one thing is guaranteed: Your broker or whoever is managing your money in the market will still get paid—a lot. The impact of 401(k) fees is colossal. According to an exposé on 60 Minutes, fees "can eat up half the income in some 401(k) plans over a thirty-year span." Yikes!

The growth you're counting on to fund your retirement can be reduced *drastically* by the fees you're paying. But most people aren't even aware of how much they're paying in fees, or they think fees are as inevitable as death and taxes.

...fees "can eat up half the income in some 401(k) plans over a thirty-year span."

Wall Street boasts about all the wonderful returns you'll earn in the stock market (if your timing and choices happen to be brilliant), but it ignores all the compounded fees and commissions you pay. *And 401(k) plans layer on even more fees*. According to the U.S. Department of Labor, if you're paying fees of only 1% and you're getting an annual 7% return, the fees alone can slash the value of your savings by 28% over the next thirty-five years. Think you're not paying 1% in fees in your 401(k)? Think again: On average, participants in small plans pay between 1.5% and 2% in fees annually, and participants in the very largest plans pay nearly 1% per year according to Brightscope, a financial information company that brings transparency to the markets. Brightscope also noted, "The sheer number of [401(k)] plans paying north of 2% a year in fees was shocking." Some plans clocked in above 3.5%!

The sheer number of [401(k)] plans paying north of 2% a year in fees was shocking.

But Didn't They Pass a Law Requiring Better Fee Disclosure?

In 2012, amidst considerable fanfare, the government passed rules designed to force 401(k) plans to disclose the fees that you're paying so you are more aware of how much you're losing to fees. The new annual disclosure form often runs more than fifteen pages, but it doesn't provide a simple figure for the annual cost you're paying. You don't get an easy-to-read summary that says, "You're paying this much for your 401(k), and here's how that compares to other plans."

It's important to know how much your plan is charging you because the growth you were hoping for is reduced each year by the fees you pay. Even with the new law requiring better fee disclosures, surveys show most participants still have *no clue* how much they're actually paying. A recent study by Ameritrade discovered that, while 95% of people surveyed knew how much they shell out for streaming media, *only 27%* had any clue how much they were paying in 401(k) fees!

What About IRA Fees?

While all the attention has been focused on the confiscatory fees you pay in a 401(k) plan, IRA fees have been ignored. Many people assume they're very low. Hold on to your wallet, because a Government Accounting Office (GAO) report blew the roof off that myth!

Have you ever left a job and rolled your 401(k) into an IRA? Millions of people do every year. Financial firms often encourage workers who are leaving a job to roll over their 401(k) assets into an IRA also managed by the firm, and many people do. However, this may be a bad move.

As recounted in the report, undercover investigators hired by the GAO called 30 of the largest 401(k) providers. Seven of these firms incorrectly stated there were *no* fees to roll over a 401(k) into an IRA and *no* ongoing fees to maintain it. And half of the ten largest firms **incorrectly** advertised "free" IRAs on their websites. The fee information was scattered in tiny print in hard-to-find documents on the site.

The study found that one of the largest IRA providers charges an annual fee of *1.5% of assets* for accounts with balances up to $500,000.

This eye-opening chart reveals how much of your retirement nest egg is devoured by the typical fees you pay in a 401(k), IRA, 403(b) or similar plan. To keep it simple, we assumed you have $100,000 in your account, earning 7% a year for 35 years:

	No fee	1% annual fee	1.5% annual fee	2% annual fee
After-fee account value after 35 years	$1,067,658	$759,776	$640,133	$538,876
Total dollars lost to fees over 35 years		-$307,882	-$427,525	-$528,782
Percent of account value lost to fees	0.0% lost	28.8% lost	40% lost	49.5% lost

Much Lower Costs Over Time in a Bank On Yourself-Type Policy

Unlike conventional retirement and investment accounts where fees are tacked on every year, ALL fees and costs for your Bank On Yourself-type dividend-paying whole life insurance policy have *already* been deducted from the projections and guaranteed values that are provided to you. This means *you can know your bottom line in advance*, with **no** surprises or smoke and mirrors.

You've probably heard it said (and you typically hear this from investment advisors) that whole life insurance commissions are high. But here's the shocking truth about high-cash value, dividend-paying whole life policies commissions as compared to investment accounts: If you put $10,000 a year for 30 years into an investment account and the market has moderate returns, *your money manager will make about $100,000* (*if* you're lucky enough to be paying an annual fee of just 1%).

But when you put $10,000 a year for 30 years into a Bank On Yourself-type policy, the commission totals around *just $8,500* over the next 30 years.

How Much Would You Rather Pay?

The projections and guaranteed values of Bank On Yourself-type policies have already had *all* costs—including insurance costs and commissions—deducted and accounted for. The bottom line you see when you sign up for a Bank On Yourself policy is *precisely* what you'll actually attain, so you know in advance the true value of your plan *at any point in time*.

Bank On Yourself lets you benefit from the magic of *compounding returns*, rather than having your nest egg severely eroded by the tyranny of *compounding costs*.

Time to Rescue Your Retirement!

Now that you're aware of the five wealth-killing traps of conventional retirement plans like 401(k)s, IRAs, 403(b)s and Roth plans—unpredictability, little or no control over your nest egg, limited access to your money when you need it, the potential tax bomb waiting for you, high fees eating away at your money—don't you think it's time to break away from the pack and look into something different?

As Marshall Thurber noted, "All the dogs barking up the wrong tree don't make it the right one!"

CHAPTER EIGHT

A Bank On Yourself Retirement

"You will observe with concern how long a useful truth may be known and exist before it is generally received and practiced on."

—BENJAMIN FRANKLIN

SO WHAT does it look like to have a Bank On Yourself retirement? We've put together a couple of case studies based on real people who have chosen to avoid the wealth-destroying traps of government-sponsored retirement plans and now bank on themselves to secure their retirement. (We've changed the names and some details to protect privacy.)

Every Bank On Yourself policy is tailored to individual goals, objectives, and circumstances. But reviewing these examples can give you a sense of how Bank On Yourself retirement savings strategies work in real life, and how that compares to the path that conventional "wisdom" would have you follow.

Case Study #1: Dentist Maximizes Her Retirement Income While Minimizing Taxes and Gaining Peace of Mind

Dr. Jane Howard is a single mom who has a small dental practice. At 46, she knows she has to get serious about saving for retirement and has been considering starting a government-sponsored tax-deferred plan to fund her retirement. She estimates she can sock away $80,000 a year (before taxes) for 20 years, until age 66 when she plans to retire.

John, her financial planner, told her that deferring taxes until retirement would help grow her money faster. (NOT TRUE! We dispelled that myth in Chapter 6.) John also mentioned that her money would be exposed to market volatility, but commented, "That's okay since the market goes up in the long run." (He didn't mention what would happen if a major market crash wiped out half of Jane's nest-egg right before she planned to retire.)

Jane told her financial planner about some scary statistics: She had read on the American Dental Association website that one in four dentists will become disabled for a lengthy period before retirement and that 75% of dentists will suffer a disorder that affects their ability to practice. Her planner then suggested she buy a disability income insurance policy that would cost her $2,400 per year and would pay her $16,500 a year to help keep food on the table until she can work again.

Jane's mother has late-stage Alzheimer's, and Jane knows this disease can run in families. She worries about how she would pay for long-term care if she suffers a similar fate. Her financial planner suggested that she buy a long-term-care policy that would pay her a $10,000 a month benefit for up to 5 years. This would cost her $3,300 a year.

Also, because she's the only income earner in the family, she wants to be able to provide for her kids in the event of her untimely death. Her planner proposed she buy a $1.5 million 20-year term life policy which would cost $2,815 a year.

If Jane implements the plan John suggested, including purchasing the disability income, long-term care, and term life policies to help address her concerns, and *if* she is able to get a 7% annual return in the market for the next 20 years while she's still working (and a more conservative 3% during her retirement years), and if she pays a typical 1.5% management fee, she could have an after-tax income of $82,186 starting at age 66 and continuing until she's age 94. She'd have to take less income at age 95 and would run out of money that year, leaving only Social Security to live on. Unfortunately, until her retirement plan income ran out, her Social Security benefit would be taxed at the highest rate, which would reduce her annual income from more than $82,000 to less than $75,000. And all of this assumes that tax rates do not increase in the future (the odds of which are slim to none, as we showed in Chapter 6).

Jane was still thinking about implementing this strategy—in spite of its uncertainties if the market crashes and the possibility of leaving her with only Social Security—when another dentist introduced Jane to her Bank On Yourself Authorized Advisor, Tim, who showed her how she could cover *all* her needs and achieve her goals using a Bank On Yourself-type policy. On top of that, her retirement income could last longer, she wouldn't have to worry about higher tax rates later on, *and* she'd be able to leave a legacy for her children— something she couldn't do with the government-sponsored plan John had proposed.

Jane was surprised when this Bank On Yourself Advisor explained that he could add a rider to a dividend-paying whole life policy that would cover her minimum premium payments in the event she became disabled. She could even borrow against the equity in her policy to get by if she became temporarily disabled. Tim also described an Accelerated Death Benefit rider that would allow Jane to access $1 million or more of her death benefit *during her lifetime* to pay for the care she would need if she developed Alzheimer's or any other chronic or terminal illness.

Bottom Line: With a Bank On Yourself-type policy, Jane could have peace of mind and guaranteed, predictable growth and enjoy a *tax-free* income in retirement of $75,000 each year from her policy until she's in her late 90s (based on the current dividend scale).

This might sound similar to the income she could get from John's plan, but with the Bank On Yourself strategy, Jane would receive several *additional* benefits:

- She could *still* have a $248,743 income tax-free death benefit left in her late 90s for her children and/or favorite charity.
- The income she takes from the policy will *not* cause her Social Security benefits to be taxed and *won't* cause her to pay the higher Medicare premiums she would have had to pay with John's plan. (Income from conventional retirement plan withdrawals can increase your Medicare premiums by as much as 350%!)
- And with the riders Tim recommended, Jane wouldn't have to worry about a disability or chronic illness scuttling her best-laid plans.

Case Study #2: Nearing Retirement and Concerned About Higher Taxes and Out-Living His Money

Tom Justice is a 59-year-old chemical engineer who loves his career and wants to continue working as long as he can. Among other assets, he has $750,000 in his 401(k) which he can soon start accessing without owing any early withdrawal penalties (though, of course, he will pay income taxes on all the money he withdraws).

Tom is concerned about the Required Minimum Distributions (RMDs) he'll have to start taking in his early 70s. He believes tax rates are going up over the long term and is worried about the big tax bite he'll be facing at that time. He is also very concerned about how to make sure his money lasts as long as he does.

His Bank On Yourself Authorized Advisor had a creative solution based on Tom's goals and objectives: Tom could roll his 401(k) balance into a fixed indexed IRA annuity, with a "guaranteed lifetime income rider." Tom could take annual withdrawals from his annuity and use this money to fund a Bank On Yourself-type policy. Doing this could reduce his RMD problem and his future tax burden. And Tom could also create an income stream he wouldn't outlive.

Here's how it works:

Step 1: Tom transfers the $750,000 in his 401(k) into an IRA fixed indexed annuity.

Step 2: The following year, Tom activates the increasing income rider feature on his annuity and withdraws $34,718 that year. With this rider on his annuity, Tom could have income that increases over time. Each increase would be locked in, and the income from his annuity would never be reduced below its highest amount.

Step 3: Tom pays 25% of the first year's withdrawal of $34,718 in income taxes that he had deferred, leaving him $26,039. Tom is still working as he planned and doesn't need the money to live on, so he uses the money to fund the first year's premium for a Bank On Yourself-type policy.

Step 4: The policy he purchases is called a "10-pay" policy, meaning that after 10 years no more premiums are required. These policies make sense for anyone with a relatively short time horizon to reach a goal or who doesn't want to be committed to paying premiums beyond 10 years. People often start these policies as late as age 55 to 65 or even older, because you're rarely "too old" to benefit from starting a whole life policy.

Step 5: After Tom funds his policy for 10 years with income he takes each year from his annuity, no more premiums are due.

Step 6: When Tom turns 70, he could start taking an *additional* $15,000 a year from the whole life policy until he's nearly 100 years old(!), with *no* taxes due under current tax law.

Step 7: Due to the increasing income rider on Tom's annuity, the income he takes from it could potentially grow to $58,108 a year by the time he's 70. When added to the $15,000 income he could take from his Bank On Yourself-type policy (based on current dividends), his total income could be $73,108 a year—*plus* he'd have Social Security. And the income he takes from his policy does *not* subject him to taxation on his Social Security benefit.

Step 8: Tom could enjoy an increasing income from the annuity—even if he lives to age 105 or beyond—which gives him the peace of mind he craves.

Bottom Line: By age 96, Tom could receive a total of $3,980,700. This is $2.5 million *more* than he would have received had he left the money in his 401(k), conservatively invested in the market earning 5% a year (since he's close to retirement, he would have avoided aggressive investments), paid a typical management fee, and started taking RMDs when required (paying taxes on those withdrawals at the then-current tax rates.)

Tom is a happy camper knowing that he no longer has to worry about RMDs pushing him into a higher tax bracket or that he'll outlive his money!

These examples give you a sense of how flexible the Bank On Yourself strategy is and how it can be customized for each individual, their unique situation, and their specific goals. Literally, *hundreds* of factors are taken into consideration when building a Bank On Yourself-type policy, and no two are alike. Though the numbers and results shown here are downright thrilling to Jane and Tom, the most *important* numbers are those that could apply to *your* situation, goals and dreams.

In the next chapter, I'll explain how you can take the next steps to get started and find out if adding the Bank On Yourself strategy to your financial plan makes sense for your situation. You can also request a *free, no-obligation* Analysis at **www.BankOnYourself.com/free-analysis.**

CHAPTER NINE

Retirement Dream or Retirement Nightmare?

"The Bank On Yourself strategy puts preparing for retirement on auto-pilot. It's like a Swiss Army Knife—it has so much flexibility and so many uses. It's the Holy Grail of financial products and strategies and makes financial independence easy."

—BOB CHAMBERS, Retired Naval Commander

HAVE YOU ever heard someone refer to their IRA or 4101(k) as "the Holy Grail?" Me neither. And by now, it should be clear why. With a conventional retirement plan, you have:

- Absolutely *no way* to predict how much money you'll have during your retirement
- *Little to no control* over the money in your retirement account
- *Little or no access* to the money in your account when you need it
- A *potential tax bomb* of higher taxes to pay on that money when you take withdrawals
- *High fees* that eat away at your account like locusts year after year

There's a good reason (actually, *several* good reasons) why the Father of the 401(k) has disowned his child!

By contrast, the Bank On Yourself strategy gives you real retirement security. Before you even decide if you want to move forward with the Bank On Yourself strategy, you know *the exact minimum amount* of money you'll have—*guaranteed*—at any point in time. You can know how much you will have in your policy ten years from now and 45 years from now. You can be confident making decisions about when you want to retire, how you want to live, and where you want to live. The only thing that's unpredictable is how much *better* you might do than the guaranteed growth, based on the dividends you could also receive!

Do you really need the stress of your conventional plan's uncertainty? You're already facing the unknowns of how long you'll live in retirement (likely longer than you thought), medical costs you'll incur in retirement (definitely more than you'd hoped), how big your tax bill will be (potentially *much* higher than you bargained for) and how inflation will reduce your future buying power in retirement (more drastically than you figured). On top of their other shortcomings, conventional retirement plans do *nothing* to address these concerns.

Bank On Yourself does.

Besides being a proven, predictable, guaranteed alternative to conventional retirement plans, the Bank On Yourself strategy offers the "Swiss Army Knife" flexibility Navy Commander Bob Chambers mentioned above. A Bank On Yourself-type policy is tailored to *your* unique current and future needs, and it can serve multiple purposes. You can use your Bank On Yourself policy for any use you can imagine. Some of the most common ways are:

- Create a substantial safe and liquid emergency fund you can tap quickly with no hassle

- Pay for trips, weddings, orthodontia, roofs, new cars—all without maxing out credit cards or begging for loans from your banker
- Start up or grow a business without having to take out bank loans
- Fund a child's or grandchild's college education without sacrificing your own retirement security
- Help protect the ones you love in the event of your death
- Leave an income tax-free legacy to your family, place of worship or favorite causes

Thanks to all the *living benefits* your Bank On Yourself policy provides, not only can you rest easy that your retirement funds are in safe hands with guaranteed, predictable growth, but you are able to access your equity in your policy for a myriad of other financial needs before you even hit retirement.

Caution! Beware of Untrained Advisors

Bank On Yourself is not an off-the-shelf type of product. To get the most out of the Bank On Yourself strategy, you need a *trained and qualified* life insurance professional who has been thoroughly educated in how to properly structure your policy to ensure you receive **all** the benefits, growth, and protections. If the wrong company or product is used or your policy is structured incorrectly, your policy could grow *much* more slowly, or you could lose some of the tax advantages, or *both*.

Too many advisors aren't willing to take a 50% or more pay cut to structure your policy to maximize the growth of your cash value. Instead, they will steer you to a higher commission product that doesn't have all of the guarantees and advantages Bank On Yourself-type policies have.

The details of how these policies are structured to maximize the power of the Bank On Yourself concept are not covered in standard industry training programs taken by agents seeking licenses. Only a handful of companies offer policies that meet all the requirements. Even most experienced planners and agents require *at least* one year of additional specialized training in this concept to become truly proficient at it.

Unfortunately, most financial advisors and insurance agents don't know what they don't know about Bank On Yourself. A little knowledge really can be a dangerous thing—and we've seen that limited knowledge produce some painful results. Prior to the creation of the Bank On Yourself Authorized Advisor training program, I spent more than 40 hours trying to fix a mistake an agent had made structuring two policies for my husband and me—even though he swore up and down he knew how to do it correctly. I wouldn't wish that experience on anyone!

How to Find a Qualified Advisor

Today, there are approximately 200 highly qualified professionals across the U.S. and Canada who form the core of Bank On Yourself Authorized Advisors. Each is a licensed life insurance agent who has undergone many hours of additional training on the technical aspects that make these policies such a powerful financial tool. As part of this training, agents learn how to coach their clients to become their own source of financing for all their needs in every stage of life, while maximizing their retirement income and minimizing their taxes in the process.

Each of these 200 Authorized Advisors:

- Has passed rigorous testing and demonstrated his/her competency with the concept
- Takes continuing education classes
- Works under the guidance of a Bank On Yourself technical and policy-design specialist team that has collectively designed tens of thousands of policies

- Is trained on creative solutions for helping you find the funds to start your policy
- Works with some of the financially strongest life insurance groups in the country, and knows which companies have policies that meet *all* the requirements needed to maximize the power of the concept
- Is willing to take a 50% or more commission cut to structure your policy to your benefit

(If you're interested in a fulfilling career as a Bank On Yourself Authorized Advisor, you can learn more about the Program and see if you qualify at **www.BankOnYourself.com/become-an-advisor.**)

What's the Next Step?

> "The best time to plant a tree is twenty years ago. The second best time is today."
>
> —ANCIENT PROVERB

You might be tempted to put this book aside and "think about it all tomorrow." Tackling your retirement challenges head-on can be daunting. But "tomorrow" can turn into weeks, months and years of staying on a path that leads to a place you never wanted to end up. I would hate to have you wake up fifteen years from now, worrying about your finances and thinking, "Heck. I should have looked into that Bank On Yourself thing." I urge you to take action *today* and take a look at this strategy that has helped so many people reach their retirement goals and attain financial peace of mind. Those folks used their best judgment and took the path less traveled to achieve the financial security that they and their families deserved.

To take the next step, request a free Analysis at **www.BankOnYourself.com/free-analysis** or complete and send in the form on the last page of this book. You'll receive a referral to an Authorized Advisor who will contact you by phone or e-mail within two business days to review your unique situation and goals and help you determine if this strategy makes sense for your situation.

As a bonus, the Bank On Yourself Authorized Advisor you're referred to will also provide you with two valuable custom reports for free:

Report #1. How to Maximize Your Social Security Benefit (a $149.00 value): The timing of when you start taking your Social Security benefits is critically important—and typically irrevocable. This report reviews the many factors that determine the best age to start taking Social Security and applies them to your unique situation to analyze the most beneficial timing and strategy for you.

Report #2. How Much Retirement Income Can You Count On? (a $199.00 value): This customized report will calculate any income shortfall—or surplus—you can expect in retirement based on where you are today.

Saving for a Comfortable and Financially Stress-Free Retirement Made Easy

The majority of this book discusses the traps of conventional retirement plans—those very plans that you, like most Americans, probably have based your financial future on. But I've also shown you a *time-tested and proven* alternative in Bank On Yourself. So let's sum it all up in a simple comparison chart that doesn't require a Stanford MBA to understand:

Which Strategy...	401(k)s, 403(b)s, etc.	IRAs	Roth Plans	Bank On Yourself
Gives you guaranteed growth	–	–	–	✓
Locks in your principal and growth	–	–	–	✓
Gives you control of your money	–	–	–	✓
Lets you use your money without penalties	–	–	–	✓
Gives you tax-free retirement income	–	–	✓	✓
Allows you to access without liquidating	–	–	–	✓
Finishes funding if you die early	–	–	–	✓
Lets you know its guaranteed value in advance	–	–	–	✓

With traditional government-sponsored retirement plans, you have surrendered control to the government and Wall Street. You can never have confidence that the next market crash won't wipe out 50% or more of your life's savings. You cannot easily determine all the fees and expenses you're paying, and over time, those fees and expenses will dramatically reduce the size of your retirement nest egg. Bank On Yourself-type policies, on the other hand, remove all the mystery by clearly stating your *guaranteed* bottom-line results *after* taking *all* fees and expenses into account.

Summing It All Up

There are *at least* eight reasons Bank On Yourself makes an excellent alternative to conventional retirement plans:

1. **Guaranteed, predictable growth and retirement income**—with **no** luck, skill, or guesswork required.

2. **No volatility.** Your policy doesn't lose value when the markets tumble. Your principal and growth are locked in. They're not subject to market risks.

3. **You're in control.** You have control of your money without government penalties or restrictions on how much income you can take or when you can take it.

4. **Tax advantages.** You can access your principal and growth with **no** taxes due, under current tax law.

5. **Liquidity.** Your cash value can easily and immediately be tapped for any purpose at all, and your policy can continue growing as though you never touched a dime of it.

6. **Fees don't compound against you.** With a Bank On Yourself-type policy, *all* costs have *already* been deducted from the bottom-line numbers you'll be provided.

7. **Income tax-free legacy.** The death benefit is likely to be many times larger than the total amount you've paid into your policy, and many times larger than your cash value. This passes to your loved ones and/or favorite charities income tax-free and without going through probate. If you die prematurely, the death benefit can essentially finish funding your savings goals to provide for your family as you had intended.

8. **Peace of mind.** Perhaps the best reason of all: You'll know the minimum guaranteed value of your nest egg on the day you plan to tap into it—and at *every* point along the way!

> **"I'm using Bank On Yourself as a source of financing, savings and financial security. And anyone who wants some economic sanity in their life ought to think about doing the same. My only regret is that I wish I had learned about this sooner."**
>
> —D.J. SIMON, IT Consultant

Like D.J. Simon, the biggest regret I hear from many people who have adopted the Bank On Yourself strategy is that they didn't get started sooner. Don't make that your regret. Don't let your inaction turn your retirement dreams into retirement nightmares. Take the next step towards economic sanity today and request a free Analysis at **www.BankOnYourself.com/free-analysis** or complete and send in the form on the last page of this book.

References

1 DALBAR 2019 Quantitative Analysis of Investor Behavior

2 Do Low-Income Workers Benefit from 401(k) Plans? September 2011 Working Paper

3 Source: Analysis of federal data by the Swartz Center for Economic Policy Analysis

4 Assuming a 40% equity portfolio. – Morningstar: Low Bond Yields and Safe Portfolio Withdrawal Rates, Blanchett, Finke & Pfau

5 U.S. Department of Health and Human Services

6 Genworth: Compare Long Term Care Costs Across the United States

7 Integrated Policy Use Microdata Series, Current Population Survey 2018

8 Economic Policy Institute: Top 1% Reaches Highest Wages Ever, Oct. 18, 2018

General Disclaimer

While a great deal of care has been taken to provide accurate and current information regarding the subject matter covered, neither Bank On Yourself nor Pamela Yellen is responsible for any errors or omissions, or for the results obtained from the use of this information. The ideas, suggestions, general principles and conclusions presented here are subject to local, state and federal laws and regulations and revisions of same, and are intended for informational purposes only. All information in this book is provided "as is," with no guarantee of completeness, accuracy, or timeliness regarding the results obtained from the use of this information, and without warranty of any kind, express or implied, including but not limited to warranties of performance, merchantability, and fitness for a particular purpose. Your use of this information is at your own risk. You assume full responsibility and risk of loss resulting from the use of this information. Pamela G. Yellen and Bank On Yourself will not be held liable for any direct, special, indirect, incidental, consequential, or punitive damages or any other damages whatsoever, whether in an action based upon a statute, contract, tort (including, but not limited to, negligence), or otherwise, relating to the use of this information. In no event will Pamela Yellen, her related partnerships or corporations, or the partners, agents, or employees thereof be liable to you or anyone else for any decision made or action taken in reliance on the information in this book or for any consequential, special, or similar damages, even if advised of the possibility of such damages. Neither Pamela Yellen nor Bank On Yourself is engaged in rendering legal, accounting, or other professional services. If accounting, financial, legal, or tax advice is required, the services of a competent professional should be sought.

Information that was accurate as of the time of publication may become outdated by marketplace changes or conditions, new or revised laws, or other circumstances. Any slights against individuals, companies, or organizations are unintentional.

About the Author

Financial security expert Pamela Yellen investigated more than 450 savings and retirement planning products and strategies seeking an alternative to the risk and volatility of stocks and other investments. Her research led her to a time-tested, predictable method of growing and protecting wealth now used by more than half a million people. Pamela has written two *New York Times* best-selling books.

Pamela has appeared on every major TV and radio network and served as a source for thousands of organizations and publications, such as the Associated Press, Fox News, *Bloomberg Businessweek, Aging Today*, and AARP.

Pamela was born in Buffalo, New York, and has lived in Sarasota, Phoenix, and the San Francisco Bay area. She graduated from the University of San Francisco with a degree in psychology. Pamela and her husband Larry currently live outside of Santa Fe, New Mexico. They enjoy theatre and the arts, hiking, jazz and rock-and-roll music, bird watching, traveling, gourmet cooking, working out, and reading, and are involved in supporting numerous charitable causes.

To learn more about Pamela Yellen and Bank On Yourself, go to **www.BankOnYourself.com**.

Free No-Obligation Analysis Request Form

Yes! I want to find out how to take back control of my financial future, grow wealth I can predict and count on and become my own source of financing. Please have a Bank On Yourself Authorized Advisor contact me, so I can receive my free, no- obligation Bank On Yourself Analysis. I understand there will be *no* high pressure and I will not be asked to buy anything during this meeting. (Note: Plese **use black ink** for readability.)

Name: ______________________________

Address: ______________________________

City: ______________ State: ________ Zip: ______________

Day Phone: ______________ Eve Phone: ______________

Primary Email Address: ______________________________

Best time to speak briefly during business hours: ______________

NOTE: We *never* trade, rent, sell, or abuse your contact or other personal information. We ask for email and phone to make it easy to put you in contact with the Bank On Yourself Advisor we refer you to, who will prepare your Analysis. By giving us this information, you authorize Bank On Yourself and the Advisor we select for you to contact you regarding your analysis.

Please tell us about you—this information will be held in **strict confidence**:

	You	*Spouse or Significant Other*
Age:	______________	______________
Occupation:	______________	______________
Annual Income:	______________	______________

Your biggest financial concern: ______________________________

Do you own your home? ________ Approx. mortgage balance: ______________

Approx. credit card debt: ________ Interest rates: ______________

Do you own a business? ________ If so, what type? ______________

How did you hear about Bank On Yourself? ______________________________

If you learned from someone, please list their name and state: ______________

To arrange for your free Bank On Yourself Analysis:

FAX this form to **505-466-2167** (no cover sheet necessary)

Or MAIL this form to: 903 W. Alameda St., #526, Santa Fe, NM, 87501

Or request it online at: **www.BankOnYourself.com/free-analysis**